THE AMAZING BOOK

AT HOME

THE AMAZING BOOK OF FIRSTS

AT HOME

Written by David Smith & Sue Cassin

Illustrated by Kim Blundell

Edited by Catriona Macgregor

COLLINS

CONTENTS

HOME ENTERTAINMENT MACHINES
p. 6-7

A collection of firsts from the world of TV, video and recorded music.

INDOOR GAMES AND PASTIMES
p. 8-9

Find out about the clever people who invented darts, snooker, chess and other popular games.

TOYS
p. 10-11

The tale of the teddy bear, and other stories of firsts from the toybox!

FURNISHINGS
p. 12-13

The alarum bedstead, the clockwork crib and other amazing furniture firsts.

IN THE KITCHEN
p. 14-15

The dishwasher discovery, the iron invention and the oven original, amongst other kitchen firsts.

IN THE BATHROOM
p. 16-17

A soapy section of bathroom firsts, such as the original sponge, shower, razor and toothbrush.

EVERYDAY ITEMS
p. 18-19

The first zip, nappy pin and light bulb are amongst these bright ideas for everyday use.

MORE EVERYDAY ITEMS
p. 20-21

More facts about everyday objects we take for granted, including the first sticky tape, ballpoint pen, rubber and lead pencil.

FOOD
p. 22-23

The first hamburgers, crisps, and other scrumptious food firsts.

DRINKS
p. 24-25

A cocktail of fizzy firsts, from the monk who invented champagne to the medicine that became the world's most popular drink!

TOOLS
p. 26-27

Egyptian saws, Chinese wheelbarrows and French spanners are amongst this set of firsts from the toolbox.

RICHES FROM THE EARTH
p. 28-29

The first diamonds and other sparkling nuggets of information about the riches of the earth.

HOME ENTERTAINMENT MACHINES

T.V. BRIBE—In 1926 a Scotsman, John Logie Baird, gave the first public demonstration of television in his workroom at Frith Street, London. The first person to be seen on television was a fifteen-year-old boy called William Taynton, who had to be bribed with money before he would stand in front of the camera.

RADIO BROADCASTING—The first regular radio broadcasting service was begun in 1920 by Westinghouse's Station KDKA in Pittsburg, Pennsylvania.

In 1954 the first transistor was developed by Regency Electronics of Indianapolis. It weighed 339g and measured 7.5cm × 12.7cm × 3.1cm.

VIDEO VENTURE—The first video cassette recorder for home use was the Philips 1500, which was launched in an exhibition at London's Olympia in 1971. In 1975 two Japanese companies (Sony and JVC) launched their own models—'Betamax' and 'Video Home System' respectively.

In 1988 Sony brought out the first personal video 'Walkman'. Pre-recorded films in colour can now be watched anywhere!

FAVOURITE MUSIC—In 1935 AEG of West Germany produced the first modern cassette player, but in 1963 Philips of Holland introduced the cassette recorder. This used a much more practical, small cassette instead of reels of tape.

In 1979 people were able to walk about and travel whilst listening to their favourite music through headphones when Sony brought out their personal stereo tape recorder called the 'Walkman'.

RECORD REVOLUTION—The first flat discs were invented in 1888 by a Mr Berliner, a German immigrant, but the first long-playing records were developed in 1948 by Dr Peter Goldwark and a research team at the Columbia Broadcasting System, USA. These records are the ones we use today and they revolve at 33.3 rpm. The 'singles' records were brought out shortly after this and revolve at 45 rpm.

The compact disc audio system was introduced in 1980 by Sony and Philips of Holland.

T.V. WATCH—The first flat-screen pocket television was introduced simultaneously in 1984 by Sony, Seiko and Casio of Japan. A wristwatch television followed shortly afterwards!

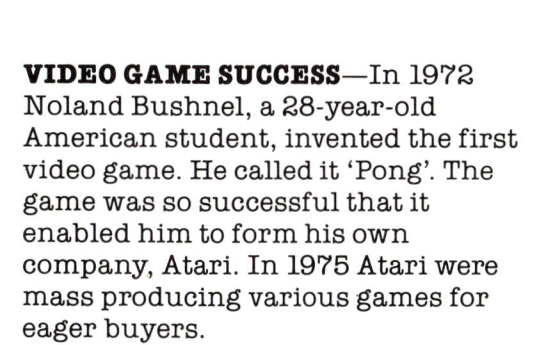

VIDEO GAME SUCCESS—In 1972 Noland Bushnel, a 28-year-old American student, invented the first video game. He called it 'Pong'. The game was so successful that it enabled him to form his own company, Atari. In 1975 Atari were mass producing various games for eager buyers.

INDOOR GAMES AND PASTIMES

WAR GAME—Chess is derived from *chaturanga*, an Indian war game, which dates from about AD 500, but the game didn't reach Europe until the 10th century. The game of chess may actually be much older, for two ivory chessmen, dating from AD 200 were found in Russia in 1972.

BILLIARDS KING—The first known game of billiards was in France in 1429. King Louis XI, who ruled France from 1461 to 1483, was the first king to have had his own billiards table!

SCRABBLE SALES—It took Alfred Butts, an architect from Connecticut, fifteen years to develop the game of 'Scrabble'. In 1946 he began making 200 sets per week at his home because games-makers thought that it was too dull to sell.

ARMY ACTIVITY—Snooker was invented in 1875 by British Army Officers serving in Southern India. They were bored with billiards so they invented another game. Its name was taken from the word 'snookers' referring to first-year cadets at the Royal Military Academy, London.

PILGRIMS' PASTIME—It is said that the game of darts was played on the *Mayflower* by the Plymouth pilgrims sailing to America in 1620. The modern game dates from about 1896 when Brian Gamlin of Bury in England, invented the way the numbers are arranged on the board.

EGYPTIAN ENTERTAINMENT—Draughts has earlier beginnings than chess. It is known to have been played by the Egyptians in as far back as 1000 BC.

TRIVIAL TRIUMPH—'Trivial Pursuit' was first launched in 1981. It was the idea of three Canadians—John and Chris Haney, and Scott Abbott.

CROSSWORD FIRST—The first crossword puzzle was compiled by Liverpool-born Arthur Wynne and appeared in the *New York World* on 21 December 1913.

BEST SELLER—'Monopoly' was invented in the 1930s by an out-of-work heating engineer, Charles Darrow. It has since grown to become the most successful of board games—by 1988 more than 85 million sets had been sold worldwide!

JIGSAW MAPS—The first jigsaw puzzle was made in 1793 by a London engraver and cartographer, John Spilsbury. He started by pasting his maps to thick wooden blocks which he cut into pieces. When all the pieces were put together they made up a map.

TOYS

TALKING DOLL—The first talking doll was made in 1823 by a German, Johann Maelzel. It said two words—*Maman* and *Papa*.

DOLLS' HOUSE BUILDERS—The first dolls' house was made by craftsmen in 1558 especially for the daughter of Duke Albrecht V of Bavaria.

LEAD LIFE GUARDS—The first model soldiers made of hollow-cast lead were a 'Life Guards' set, produced by Britain's of Great Britain in 1893. The first plastic model soldiers were 'US Infantrymen'. They were marketed by Betch Toys, New Jersey, in 1938.

LEGO LAUNCH—Lego was invented by Godtfred Kirk Christiansen in 1955. He used interlocking plastic toy bricks he developed with his father, Ole Kirk Christiansen, a Danish carpenter and joiner. *Leg godt* is Danish for 'play well' and *lego* is Latin for 'put together'.

ROLLER SKATE CRASH—Roller skates were invented in 1760 by Joseph Merlin from Huy, Belgium. He was a violinist and wore his two-wheeled skates at a Masquerade ball in London. He skated into the ballroom playing his violin, but unfortunately he smashed a valuable mirror and wounded himself badly!

The first four-wheeled roller skates were made in 1863 by a Mr Plimton from New York.

SKATEBOARD SENSATION—Skateboards were first used in California in 1966. They were improved in 1973 by using urethane plastic wheels. This was the idea of Frank Nasworthy, also from California.

CLOCKWORK TRAIN—In 1856 George Browne, a watchmaker from Connecticut, made the first clockwork train.

The first model train set with complete track layout also worked by clockwork. It was made in 1891 by Märklin Brothers of Göppingen, West Germany.

TOY ELEPHANT—The first soft toy was a felt elephant made by Margarete Steiff from Giengen in West Germany in 1880.

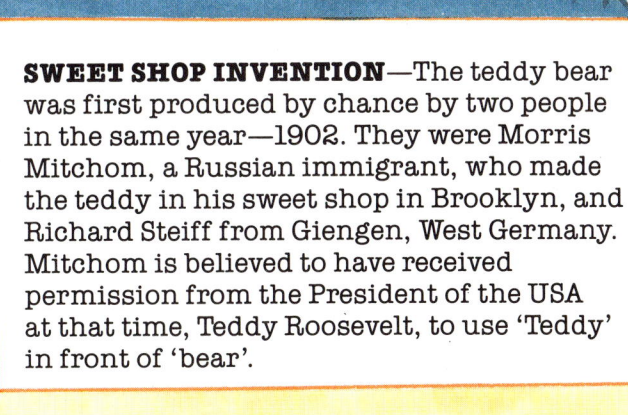

SWEET SHOP INVENTION—The teddy bear was first produced by chance by two people in the same year—1902. They were Morris Mitchom, a Russian immigrant, who made the teddy in his sweet shop in Brooklyn, and Richard Steiff from Giengen, West Germany. Mitchom is believed to have received permission from the President of the USA at that time, Teddy Roosevelt, to use 'Teddy' in front of 'bear'.

FURNISHINGS

TIP-UP BED—Couch-like beds existed in Egypt as early as 2500 BC. The ancient Greeks and Romans used them to recline on whilst eating their meals and also to sleep on at night. Until the 17th century, beds were only used and owned by the wealthy and powerful.

In about 1850 a bizarre 'alarum bedstead' was invented in Great Britain. One of its features included an alarm clock on the bedhead—when the bell finished ringing, the front legs of the bed folded gently and the person in bed was tipped onto his or her feet!

CARPET COMFORT—The first carpets were hand-knotted and made in Iran or China in about 600 BC. Carpets were first woven on looms in the seventeenth century, in France.

VENETIAN IDEA—In 1769 Edward Bevan, from England, devised Venetian blinds (window coverings made of thin slats which can be raised or lowered to allow light or air into a room). Bevan called them 'Venetian blinds' because he first thought of the idea when he was in Venice.

WALLPAPER DISCOVERY—The first known wallpaper was discovered at the Master's Lodgings, Christ's College, Cambridge during the course of rebuilding in 1911. The wallpaper itself is believed to date from 1509. It was made of small sheets, printed with floral patterns from a wood block and was made by Hugo Goes of York.

ALARMING TEA-MAKER—The automatic tea-maker was invented in 1902 by Frank Clarke, a gunsmith from Birmingham. The machine was set off by an alarm clock which worked levers and springs to strike its own match and light a spirit stove. It would then boil a small kettle of water, tip it up when ready to pour into the teapot, and strike the alarm bell!

CEREMONIAL CHAIRS—Seats with backs used to be very rare. The first high-backed chairs were used in Ancient Egypt, for special ceremonies.

PLANTS' PARADISE—In 1716 Martin Triewald, a Swedish engineer, installed the first hot water heating system to warm a greenhouse, in Newcastle-upon-Tyne.

CLOCKWORK CRIB—In 1861 a clockwork cradle-rocker was invented in Switzerland, but there is no record of it ever having been used since then.

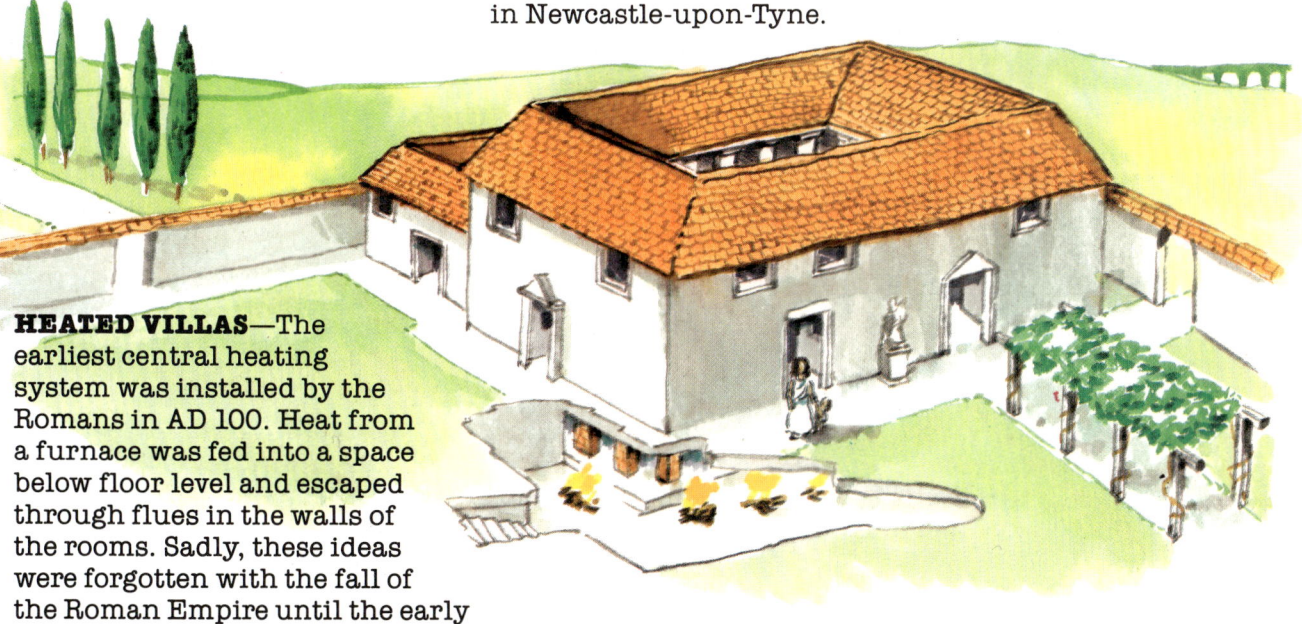

HEATED VILLAS—The earliest central heating system was installed by the Romans in AD 100. Heat from a furnace was fed into a space below floor level and escaped through flues in the walls of the rooms. Sadly, these ideas were forgotten with the fall of the Roman Empire until the early eighteenth century when central heating was revived in France and Holland.

IN THE KITCHEN

CLEAN CLOTHES—The first electric washing machine was invented in 1906 by Alva J. Fisher from Chicago, and was sold to the public in 1910 as the 'Thor' machine.

The first electric-powered wash and spin dry machine appeared in 1924, and was devised by Savage Arms Corporation, of New York.

IRON INVENTION— Henry Seely, from New York, invented the first electric flat iron in 1882. The steam iron appeared in 1938 and was the idea of Edmund Schreyer.

VACUUM VENTURE—In 1901 Hubert Booth from England devised the first electric vacuum cleaner. A motor drove a pump which sucked up the dirt.

The first upright vacuum cleaner with a dustbag attached was invented in 1907 by J. Murray Spangler, a janitor working in a department store in Ohio.

TOAST TIMER—The pop-up toaster was created in 1927 by Charles Strite of Minnesota. It had heating elements on both sides and a special clockwork timer which turned off the electric current.

PAN PROGRESS—The non-stick frying pan was the idea of Mark Grégoire of France. In 1958 he developed a pan coated with special plastic which is unaffected by hot or cold temperatures and is very slippery.

WONDER MACHINE—The first electric food processor was devised in 1936 by the Sunbeam Corporation, USA. It had attachments to peel, slice and liquidize fruit and vegetables.

FIRST KETTLE—Bill Russell and Peter Hobbs of Dartford invented the first automatic electric kettle in 1955. When boiling point was reached the hot steam cut off the power.

STEAM ENGINE DISHWASHER—In 1889, after 10 years of development, a power dishwasher was produced for sale by a Mrs Cockram of Indiana.

The larger models were often used in hotels and could wash, scald, rinse and dry up to 240 dishes of all shapes and sizes in just two minutes.

OVEN INVENTION—The first electric oven was installed in the Hotel Bernina, Samaden in Switzerland in 1889. The electric power supply was generated from a dynamo which was driven by a nearby waterfall.

FRIDGE FACT—The first refrigerator for household use was made in 1913 in Chicago. It had a wooden cabinet on top of which a refrigerating unit was built.

IN THE BATHROOM

BATHING DUKE—The first person to have the luxury of hot and cold running water in his bathroom was the Duke of Devonshire at his home in Chatsworth in 1700.

One of the earliest shower baths was also installed at Chatsworth in the 1840s. Water from a basin was pumped up by hand through pipes into the showerhead. The water then fell down onto the bather.

The first royal bath tub, dating from 1700 BC, was found in a Queen's bathroom at the Palace of King Minos in Knossos, Crete.

MIRACLE TOOTHBRUSH—A Chinese encyclopaedia published in the 17th century claims that the toothbrush was first invented in China in 1498.

The first modern-type toothbrush was made by a London tanner, William Addis in 1780. Addis toothbrushes are still used today.

In 1885 an American called Dr Scott devised the first electric toothbrush and in 1938 the first nylon bristle toothbrush—Dr West's 'miracle tuft toothbrush'—was marketed in the USA.

SEE-THROUGH SOAP—The earliest known recipe for soap comes from Mesopotamia and dates from 3000 BC. In 1798 Andrew Pears, a Cornish-born hairdresser working in London, made the first transparent soap. It was not, however, until 1829 that the first wrapped-up soap—James Atkinson's 'Old Brown London Soap'—was on sale.

RAZOR RECORD—The first double-edged safety razor was patented in the USA in 1901 by King Camp Gillette. Within one year a total of 90,000 Americans were using this razor and got through nearly 12½ million disposable razor blades! In 1931 the first electric razor was manufactured in Connecticut by Colonel Jacob Schick.

SPONGE SUCCESS—Natural sponges were used by the Egyptians. They used to soak them in honey and give them to their babies as dummies. In 1931 the first artificial sponge was invented by Novacel of France.

EVERYDAY ITEMS

LIGHT SUCCESS—Thomas Edison from the USA invented the electric light bulb in 1879. The bulb provided 13½ hours of light, enough for a long winter's evening.

AEROSOL IDEA—In 1926 Erik Rotheim, from Norway, found a method of propelling products such as scent, hair-lacquer and paint, from a can. It was not until 1941 that two Americans, L.D. Goodhue and W.N. Sullivan, developed this idea commercially when they sold the first aerosol—an insect-repellent spray.

SCISSORS STORY—Bronze scissors were in use in Asia and Europe as early as 1000 BC. Mass production began in 1761 and was started by Robert Hinchcliffe of Sheffield. The scissors were made of cast steel.

ZIP HITCH—The first zip fastener was devised in 1891 by Whitcomb Judson from Chicago, but was very unreliable! In 1906 Gideon Sundback, a Swedish engineer, produced a fastener using interlocking metal teeth which were drawn together by a slide. This zip was much more reliable and the design is still used today.

NAPPY-PIN—The safety-pin was devised in 1849 by an American called Walter Hunt. It had a hidden point and a coil spring.

SHORT-SIGHT SOLUTION—Spectacles were first used in Venice in about 1280. They were held in the hand but a later version—pince-nez—rested on the nose.

POLICE DUSTBIN—A Paris Prefect of Police, Eugène Poubelle, was very displeased with the amount of waste paper scattered untidily around the offices of the Préfecture of Police. In 1883 he invented the first dustbin—a galvanized iron portable container. He had several of these dustbins installed around the offices to make the rooms tidier.

WATERPROOF WONDER—Umbrellas were symbols of rank in China around 1000 BC. The frames were made of either cane or sandalwood with a covering of leaves or feathers.

The first recorded waterproof umbrellas were listed in a 1637 inventory of King Louis XIII of France. He had three umbrellas made of oiled cloth, trimmed underneath with gold and silver lace.

MORE EVERYDAY ITEMS

TREE DECORATIONS—In 1605 an unidentified visitor to Strasbourg wrote that 'for Christmas they have fir trees in their room, and decorated with paper roses, apples, sugar, gold and wafers'.

STICKY TAPE—Adhesive tape (Sellotape) was invented in 1929 by Richard Drew of the 3M Company, St Paul.

In 1934 James Chalmers of Dundee made the first adhesive postage stamps.

NON-BLOT PEN—The biro pen was devised by a Hungarian hypnotist, sculptor and journalist called Ladislao Biro. He had worked for years to make a pen which would not blot . . . Finally, in 1945 his pen was produced by Eterpen Company of Buenos Aires.

CHRISTMAS CARD CRAZE—The first Christmas card was designed in 1843 by John Calcott Horsley of Great Britain. Copies of it were sent by Sir Henry Cole to his friends. However, sending Christmas cards did not really become popular until 1862.

TICKET INSPECTORS' TORCHES—The first electric torch was square in shape and was made by the British Electric Lamp Company in 1891. Sixty examples of this model were used by ticket inspectors of the Bristol Omnibus Company in 1892.

The Electric and Novelty Company of New York, (later to be known as the Ever Ready Company), brought out the first tubular electric torch in 1898.

LEAD EATER—Mr Nairne, a mathematical instrument maker from London, invented the eraser in 1770. It was popularly called a 'rubber' or 'lead eater' because of the way 'it wiped from the paper the marks of a black-lead pencil'.

GRAPHITE PENCILS—The pencil was first described in 1565 by a Swissman, Konrad Gesner. He defined it as 'a piece of lead in a stick of wood'.

FOOD

CEREAL CRAZE—Cornflakes were first produced in 1898 by William Kellog from Battle Creek in Michigan. Today they are the most popular cereal in the world.

CHIP ACCIDENT—The first crisps were really an accident! In 1853 a Red Indian chef, George Crum, was working at the Moon Lake House Hotel, Saragota Springs. One day a diner asked him for thinner than normal French fried potatoes. They proved very popular and were known as 'Saragota chips'.

DOUGHNUT SURPRISE—Believe it or not, the first doughnuts with holes were made in 1847 by a fifteen-year-old apprentice baker, Hanson Crocket, who was working in Camden in Maine. One morning he spotted raw mixture in the centre of his fried cakes, so he cut out the middle and produced the first ring doughnuts.

LEMONADE LOLLIPOP—On a very cold night in 1905, Frank Epperson, of San Francisco, left a mixing stick in a glass of lemonade on his windowsill. In the morning the lemonade had frozen into the first iced lollipop.

HAMBURGER HUNGER—The first hamburgers were eaten by the Tartars, a Mongol people, around 1240. Their recipe for a hamburger was raw, shredded camel, goat or horsemeat made into a pâté.

GAMBLING SNACK—The first sandwich was eaten by the fourth Earl of Sandwich in 1762. The Earl was playing cards in London and was determined not to leave the gambling tables, even though he was very hungry. He ordered 'slices of beef placed between bread', and so the first sandwich was made!

ICE-CREAM DELIGHT—In the 17th century a French chef, Gerald Tissain, prepared the first ice-cream. Charles I, who was King of England at that time, was so pleased that he paid the chef £20 each year for the rest of his life.

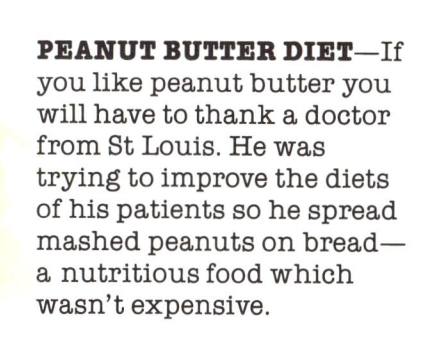

PEANUT BUTTER DIET—If you like peanut butter you will have to thank a doctor from St Louis. He was trying to improve the diets of his patients so he spread mashed peanuts on bread—a nutritious food which wasn't expensive.

DRINKS

MAGIC BERRIES—Legend tells us that around AD 850 an Abyssinian goatherd called Kaldi was very curious about the antics of his goats. They became very lively after eating the berries of an evergreen coffee bush. Kaldi decided to try some himself and found that they made him feel full of life. He met a Moslem monk who was always dozing off during prayers, so Kaldi gave him some of the berries, which kept the monk awake without any problem!

COFFEE CURE—Coffee as a drink was first recorded around AD 1000 by the Arabian philosopher and physician, Aricenna.

For centuries coffee was mainly used as a medicine. It was only in the 16th century that it was drunk socially—in Arabia and Persia.

BRAIN BEVERAGE—Coca-Cola was invented by Dr John Pemberton from Atlanta. It was launched as a 'brain tonic' in March 1886 and was first bottled in 1894 by Joseph Biedenham.

CURE FOR INDIGESTION—Pepsi-Cola was first made by the owner of a drugstore, Caleb Bradham of North Carolina, in 1898. It was devised to cure indigestion (dyspepsia), hence its name, 'Pepsi'.

HOT CHOCOLATE BEAN—Cocoa was first prepared in a powder form by Coenraad van Houten of Amsterdam in 1828. Excess cocoa butter was extracted from the crushed cacao bean.

HOLY DRAM—Whisky is attributed to St Patrick who lived in Ireland in AD 450.

The distillation of Scotch Whisky was first recorded in 1495 in the Scottish Exchequer Rolls.

Bourbon Whisky was first distilled from maize in 1789 by Rev. Elijah Craig from Bourbon County in Kentucky.

DAIRY RECORD—Milk was first sold in bottles in 1879 by the Echo Farm Dairy Company of New York.

BENEDICTINE NECTAR—Champagne was first produced in 1688 by Dom Pierre Perignon. He was a monk in charge of the cellar at the Benedictine Abbey of Hautvilliers in Champagne in France.

TEA TALE—Tea was first introduced into Europe from South East Asia by the Dutch East India Company in 1609.

It was not until 1826 that tea was first sold in packets—this was on the Isle of Wight, by John Horniman. The first tea bags were produced by Joseph Krieger from San Francisco in 1920.

TOOLS

FRENCH SPANNERS—The history of spanners is not clear, but various types were made in Italy and France to deal with nuts and bolts from about 1550 onwards. Spanners with movable jaws date from about 1700 and are sometimes known as 'French spanners'.

POMPEII TOOLS—In AD 79 the Romans used planes for smoothing wood. Examples of planes have been found amongst the ruins of Pompeii.

The first metal plane was made in 1880 by Leonard Bailey of Boston.

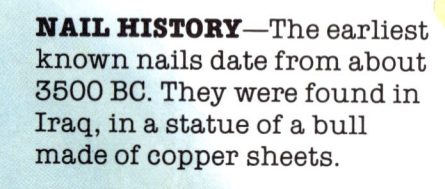

NAIL HISTORY—The earliest known nails date from about 3500 BC. They were found in Iraq, in a statue of a bull made of copper sheets.

SAW SUCCESS—The saw is one of the earliest tools of civilized man. In 3000 BC Egyptians were using saws to cut wood and stone. Saw marks can be seen on the stone of the Pyramids.

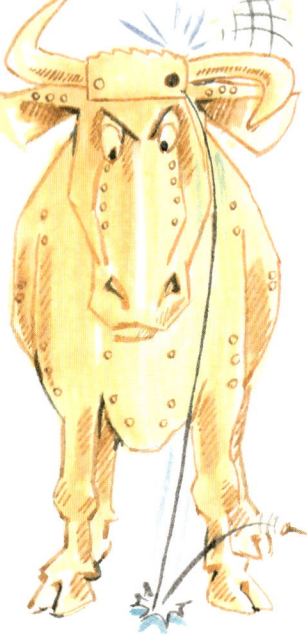

WHEELBARROW WONDER—Believe it or not, the first wheelbarrow was thought to have been in use in China as early as AD 100.

GUN GADGET—Screws were a development of the nail and first appeared in the 16th century. In about 1550 screwdrivers were known as 'turnscrews' and were used by gunsmiths and armourers to adjust their gun mechanisms.

WHEEL REPAIRER—In about 1250 a M. de Honnecourt of France illustrated the screw jack. It is a hand-operated tool and can lift and support great weights with little human effort. In the 16th century the screw jack was widely used in Germany and Holland to lift up fully loaded wagons and so repair damaged wheels.

BUDDING LAWNMOWER—Edwin Budding of Gloucester invented the first lawnmower. In 1830 he signed an agreement with John Ferrabee of the Phoenix Iron Works in Stroud for the manufacture of 'machinery for . . . shearing the vegetable surface of lawns'.

RICHES FROM THE EARTH

LAMP LIGHTER—In experiments carried out in 1792 William Murdock of Glasgow successfully lighted a house in Cornwall using coal gas, for the first time ever. The first use of natural gas was for lighting 30 street lamps in Fredonia, New York in 1821.

WATERPROOF BOAT—In around 2400 BC a form of oil called bitumen was used in Mesopotamia to make boats watertight.

SILVER FIND—Silver was one of the earliest metals to be used by man. Silver ornaments have been found in the Royal tombs in Egypt dating as far back as 4000 BC.

In 1903 Fred La Rose, a blacksmith from Ontario, threw his hammer at a roaming fox and quite by chance struck silver. The hammer landed on what turned out to be the richest vein of silver ever. He sold his claim for $30,000 and by 1913 the vein had yielded silver worth $300 million!

DIAMOND RING—Diamonds are the Earth's hardest known natural substance. They were first recorded in India in about 300 BC.

The first diamond engagement ring was made in 1477 for Archduke Maximilian, the son of the Holy Roman Emperor, Frederick III. In a gold ring diamonds were set in the shape of 'M', for Mary, his future bride.

GOLD RIVERS—Gold is one of the most precious metals and was first known in the Middle East in about 4000 BC. The earliest gold was obtained from river-beds, but during Roman times gold mines as deep as 76m were in production in Spain.

OIL FUEL—Coal was first dug up around 2000 BC in Europe. In AD 1 it was used as a fuel by the Romans in Northern Europe. By the time the 14th century arrived Great Britain had become the main coal mining country.

RADIUM DISCOVERY—Radium is a very rare, shining-white metal which is radioactive. It was discovered in 1898 by Pierre and Marie Curie of France.

COPPER ISLAND—It is believed that copper was known before 4000 BC and was the first metal used by man. The earliest evidence of copper working was a smelting site in Yugoslavia.

Copper takes its name from the Mediterranean island of Cyprus.

WROUGHT IRON—The Hittites, of Anatolia in Turkey, first produced wrought iron about 1500 BC. They burned the iron ore, which was dug from the ground, and made it as pure as possible by hammering.

29

INDEX

ball-point pens, 20
bathroom, 16-17
    bath, 16
    razor, 17
    soap, 17
    sponges, 17
    toothbrushes, 16

cassette recorder, 7
central heating, 13
Christmas firsts, 20, 21
clockwork cradle, 13

diamonds, 28
drinks, 24-5
    champagne, 25
    Coca-Cola, 24
    coffee, 24
    milk, 25
    Pepsi, 24
    tea, 25
    whisky, 25
dustbins, 19

food, 22-3
    chocolate, 25
    cornflakes, 22
    doughnuts, 22
    hamburgers, 23
    ice-cream, 23
    lollipops, 22
    peanut butter, 23
    potato crisps, 22
    sandwiches 23
furnishings, 12-13
    beds, 12
    carpets, 12
    chairs, 13

games, 8-9
    billiards, 8
    chess, 8
    crossword puzzles, 9
    darts, 9
    draughts, 9
    jigsaw puzzles, 9
    Monopoly, 9
    Scrabble, 8
    snooker, 8
    Trivial Pursuit, 9

household inventions, 14-15
    dishwashers, 15
    electric kettle, 15
    electric oven, 15
    food processor, 14
    irons, 14
    light bulbs, 18
    non-stick frying pan, 14
    refrigerator, 15
    toaster, 14
    vacuum cleaners, 14
    washing machines, 14

lawnmower, 27

metals and minerals, 28-9

pencils, 21

radio broadcasts, 6
records, 7

safety pin, 19
scissors, 18
spectacles, 19
sticky tape, 20

televisions, 6, 7
tools, 26-7
torches, 21
toys, 10-11
    clockwork trains, 11
    dolls' houses, 10
    Lego, 10
    model soldiers, 10
    roller skates, 11
    skateboards, 11
    soft toys, 11
    talking dolls, 10
    teddy bears, 11

umbrella, 19

venetian blinds, 12
videos, 6, 7

wallpaper, 12
wheelbarrows, 27